Navigating Life with Jesus

Let Jesus be your compass

in every season of life

By: Patrick J. Fischer

COPYRIGHT

Published by: Patrick J. Fischer

FischerPublishing.com

Printed in the United States

eBook ISBN: 978-0-692-04974-7

Regular print, paperback ISBN: 979-8-218-88892-3

Large print, paperback ISBN: 979-8-218-88893-0

To Kimberly—God's most beautiful gift to me on this earth,

whose love reflects the grace of His greatest gift: Jesus.

Table of Contents

Life Is Like an Empty Boat

Life is like an empty boat, set adrift the moment we take that first breath.

As infants, we rely on love and comfort only a parent can provide—gentle hands to calm the waves, soft voices to show the way. From that moment on, the waters we sail are never the same—each person's journey is shaped by different winds, different storms, and different shores.

Some boats are filled with support and grace. Others drift through hardship and silence. But every life, no matter how quiet or chaotic, carries the potential to find meaning, direction, and peace.

Life is uncertain.

Some lose loved ones much too early; their boat suddenly emptied of warmth and belonging. Some boats take on water—losing jobs, facing financial hardship, and watching dreams slip through their fingers like water. And some, through no fault of their own, find themselves without shelter, navigating the streets armed with only grit and hope.

For some, waters are calm; for others, relentless.

It is easy to envy boats that seem to glide effortlessly, untouched by storms. But every vessel has its own story, its unseen weight. And while some sailors are handed maps and anchors, others must learn to chart their course with nothing but faith and perseverance.

Yet, even in the darkest waters, light glimmers.

Kindness can be a lighthouse. Faith can be a rudder. And love—it is the wind that can move even the most battered boat forward. We are not defined by the ease of our journey but by the courage with which we sail.

So, if your boat feels empty today, know this:

You are not alone. You are not forgotten.

And the journey ahead holds beauty, purpose, and grace.

My Empty Boat

When I was seven years old, I shared a bedroom with my 19-year-old brother. He loved fast cars and racing and always seemed to chase speed and freedom. One night, he had a terrible accident—his car was a total wreck. After days in the hospital, with machines barely keeping him alive, my parents needed to face the heartbreaking decision of letting him go.

That day, we began another journey in an empty boat.

I grew up Catholic—praying before meals, attending church every Sunday, putting on our best clothes, and honoring traditions. I was baptized as a child, went to Sunday school, received communion, and confessed my sins. Looking back, I am deeply grateful that my parents honored God and the Catholic faith. They introduced me to Him early, and their devotion helped them navigate life and raise a family through joy and sorrow.

My parents owned a car wash and a gas station, and I grew up to the rhythm of the family business. By fifth grade, I was pumping gas and detailing cars—earning a paycheck and learning the value of hard work. I loved greeting customers, helping people, and proving my worth. I made sure no one ever thought things were easy for me just because I was the owner's son.

After high school, I worked alongside my father restoring cars. Through auto body work, I learned to envision the finished product even before the first stroke—an ability I continue to use today as I build brands, design websites, develop products, and lead multiple businesses. Restoring cars was my way of giving back to my father—honoring what he loved. He had spent years bringing old VW bugs back to life, and I was proud to follow in his footsteps—until it was time to take my own.

In 1983, I enrolled at the DeVry Institute of Technology to study electronics and learn about computers. This decision was a pivotal chapter in my life. For more than 30 years, I have operated a business dedicated to supporting individuals who are blind or visually impaired—providing products and services that empower independent living.

However, I wrote this book to share the greatest gift I have ever received: accepting Jesus Christ as my Savior and becoming born again in 1985. That moment changed everything: it filled my empty boat with purpose, direction, and hope.

A Note on Scripture and Purpose

Throughout this book, you will encounter references to various Bible verses—each was chosen to illuminate the paths of faith, service, and spiritual growth. I encourage you to look them up as you read, whether in your personal Bible or online at BibleGateway.com, where you can explore different translations and deepen your understanding. For consistency and clarity, all Scripture quotations in this book have been taken from the New International Version (NIV).

Walking with Jesus is more than a devotional practice—it's a daily invitation to live with purpose. The Christian life isn't just about receiving blessings; it's about becoming a blessing. When we respond to the needs of others with compassion and generosity, we reflect the heart of Christ. And in that reflection, we often find ourselves receiving exactly what we need—not always what we expect, but always what God, in His perfect wisdom, knows is best.

This book is founded on the truth that giving is a spiritual rhythm—not a transaction. It is about trusting that as you pour out, God pours in. As you lift others, He lifts you. As you walk with Jesus, you will discover that the greatest blessings frequently come through the act of helping someone else find theirs.

How Does Someone Become Born Again?

Here is a simple path that many Christians follow:

Admit—Acknowledge that you are a sinner in need of grace.

(Romans 3:23): "for all have sinned and fall short of the glory of God,"

Believe—Believe that Jesus Christ is the Son of God, sent by the Father to die for our sins and rise again, offering eternal life to all who trust in Him.

(John 3:16): "For God so loved the world that he gave his one and only Son, that whoever believes in him shall not perish but have eternal life."

Confess—Confess Jesus as Lord and Savior.

(Romans 10:9): "If you declare with your mouth, "Jesus is Lord," and believe in your heart that God raised him from the dead, you will be saved."

The phrase born again comes from a powerful moment in Scripture—Jesus' conversation with Nicodemus in (John 3:3). Jesus replied, "Very truly I tell you, no one can see the kingdom of God unless they are born again"

Thus, being saved is being born again.

Jesus is Your Spiritual Compass

The most transformative moment of my life happened in 1985, when I surrendered my heart to Jesus Christ and was born again. This decision sparked a lifelong journey of faith, and this book is a narrative of how I walk through life with Him as my guide, strength, and constant companion.

This moment transformed my life. My prayer is that, through the pages of this book, others will encounter the same life-changing love of Jesus and find their own path to renewal.

By design, this book is simple—because the path to becoming born again is not meant to be complicated—it is clear, honest, and full of grace.

In the subtitle "Let Jesus be your compass in every season of life," the term compass symbolizes guidance, direction, and clarity. Just as a physical compass helps travelers find their way—especially when a path is uncertain or unfamiliar—Jesus, as a spiritual compass, helps you navigate life's challenges, decisions, and transitions with purpose and peace.

It means trusting Jesus to guide you toward truth, love, and wisdom regardless of the season of your life—whether it involves joy, sorrow, growth, or waiting. He becomes a steady reference point when the world feels chaotic, a moral anchor when making choices is difficult, and a source of hope when the road ahead is uncertain. Letting Jesus be your compass is an invitation to walk by faith—not fear—and to let His presence lead you through every step of the journey.

Born Again–1985

In the summer of 1985, I gave my life to Jesus Christ with this prayer: "Lord Jesus, I know I've sinned, and I ask for Your forgiveness. I believe that God the Father sent You to die for our sins and offer eternal life to all who believe. You died for me and rose again. I invite You into my heart—make me new. I want to follow You and live for You. Thank You for saving me and making me born again. Amen."

That moment marked a new beginning. Before I was saved, I have been working in the computer industry since 1984, and my job had begun to feel stagnant and unfulfilling. I prayed for a new opportunity—one that would challenge me and allow me to grow.

Two days after I accepted Jesus Christ into my life, He answered my prayer in a very memorable way. My phone rang—it was the Vice President of a company who had interviewed me four months earlier and was now ready to offer me a position.

I scheduled a meeting with them the next day. During the meeting, I accepted their offer with gratitude. The same day, I also respectfully gave a notice of resignation to my current employer—expressing appreciation for the opportunities I had been given and explaining my decision to move forward into a new chapter.

For 18 unforgettable months, I had the privilege of working in commercial insertion for satellite TV—just as trailblazers such as ESPN, MTV, USA, and CNN were beginning to transform the media landscape. It was an electrifying time, and I remain deeply grateful for this prayer answered.

God then opened another door. I stepped into a new chapter—this time, as a technician in the engineering and AEC (architecture, engineering, and construction) fields, where I constructed and delivered turn-key computer systems equipped with AutoCAD, AEC software, digitizers, and plotters. It was a hands-on, high-tech role—and I prayed every step of the way for guidance.

Although my tenure was only 28 months—working 40, 50, and sometimes 60 hours per week, I had a powerful realization: with prayer and perseverance, I could do anything. That job became another testimony of God's faithfulness and the strength He gives when we follow His will by walking through doors He opens.

It is important to remember that God answers in his perfect timing, not ours. Therefore, we hold fast to our unwavering belief in the one who sent his son, Jesus Christ, to die for our sins—to have everlasting life. This is the truth we believe, the promise we live for, and the hope we carry each day.

A Calling Born From Compassion

In 1988, I launched my first company, Share Technology, with a simple mission: to use my skills as a computer technician to help people with disabilities. I walked into a neurological hospital and offered my services—no charge, just the desire to make a difference.

The first person I helped was a young boy bound to a wheelchair. His switch-controlled fan had malfunctioned. I opened the device, soldered a broken wire, and restored its function. The next moments changed my life: his mother embraced me, the nurse thanked me, and the boy beamed with joy—all igniting a fire in my heart. I knew then and there—I wanted to spend the rest of my life helping people with disabilities.

In 1997, driven by passion for accessible technology, personalized training, and lifelong support, I founded F1-Key, LLC—a company devoted to empowering individuals with blindness or visual impairment. "F1-Key" was inspired by the F1 key on Microsoft Windows, symbolizing immediate assistance and reliable guidance.

It embodied the heart of my mission and encapsulated in my original motto: "When you need help."

As the company evolved, and my vision expanded, I rebranded it in 2004 as Accessibility Dot Net, Inc. The new name reflected a broadened commitment to digital inclusion and innovation. Now, nearly three decades later, I remain dedicated to serving the blind and visually impaired community—developing tools, resources, and support systems that meet specific real-world needs. Today, my guiding principle is: "Accessibility Driven, by Demand." It is more than a motto—it is a promise to respond, adapt, and deliver solutions that truly make a difference.

Faith, Business, and the Call to Serve

Operating a small-scale business is a difficult task. On many seasons, I earned less than expected and questioned whether I should give up and find a regular job. Each time doubt crept in, I turned to God in prayer: "Lord, give me a sign. Help me make the right decision."

He always did.

I found answers not in profit margins but in people—grateful, smiling, and deeply appreciative of the help I offered. For me, it was God's way of saying, "Keep going. You are doing what I have called you to do."

Profit was not always high. I frequently reduced prices and provided free services. At one point, I had employees, multiple offices, vehicles, payroll, and taxes—yet very little was left over for myself. Nevertheless, I pressed on. Over time, I discovered meaningful success by supporting individuals with blindness, poor vision, or visual impairment. Along with this mission, I established a thriving side business as an author—writing books, crafting scripts, producing videos, and managing printing and publishing projects.

Whether organizations realize it or not, helping others is the heartbeat of every business. I hold deep respect for every company and the hardworking people within them. I love business, and I especially admire those who find joy in their work and use it to serve others.

"Do what you love, and love what you do"—I carry this prayer for everyone. Since childhood, we were told we can be anything and do anything. This truth still stands. This book was written to inspire people to be the best version of themselves and to love all people!

My hope is to encourage every reader to live with the same love, compassion, and purpose that Jesus modeled. When our work becomes an act of service, it becomes a reflection of Him.

As we journey through life, we acquire values, habits, and perspectives—shaped, in turn, by what we have seen, heard, and lived. In many ways, we become reflections of our experiences, and everyone has a story to tell. This book offers a glimpse into mine: what I have come to believe and learned along the way. It is not perfect, but it is sincere. It may not articulate everything, but it speaks from the heart.

I have kept this book short and simple, because I want everyone—regardless of background or belief—to discover Jesus and the blessings He offers. You do not need a theology degree to understand grace. You just need an open heart.

The Bible

The Bible is more than just a book—it is a sacred anthology central to Christianity and Judaism and deeply respected in other Abrahamic faiths such as Islam. Composed of 66 books in the majority of Christian traditions, it was written by more than 40 authors across approximately 1,500 years in the Hebrew, Aramaic, and Greek languages. These writings offer spiritual insight, historical context, and moral guidance that have influenced cultures and beliefs for generations.

The Bible is divided into two main sections: the Old Testament—which contains 39 books that reveal creation, laws, history, poetry, and prophecy, and the New Testament—which includes 27 books that focus on the life, teachings, death, and resurrection of Jesus Christ, along with the growth of the early church. Taken together, these books tell the story of God's relationship with humanity—from the beginning of time to the promise of eternal redemption.

The Bible tells a unified story of love, grace, and salvation—beginning with God's covenant in the Old Testament and fulfilled through Jesus in the New Testament. From the Gospels to Revelation, it reveals His message, the early church, and a victorious hope.

The Enduring Power of the Bible

Most Translated and Distributed: With more than 5 billion copies sold, the Bible remains as the most widely shared book in human history.

Global Influence: Its teachings have shaped laws, literature, ethics, and cultures across continents and over time.

A Living Text: For many, the Bible is more than a historical document—it is a timeless source of wisdom, guidance, and personal transformation.

Being born again means experiencing spiritual rebirth—a transformation of the heart through faith in Jesus Christ. It is more about receiving new life through the Holy Spirit and not about starting over physically. It is the beginning of a personal relationship with God, marked by forgiveness, renewal, and a desire to walk in His light.

Timeless Truths From the Teachings of Jesus

The wisdom of Jesus continues to inspire hearts and shape lives across cultures and generations. His words offer more than spiritual insight—they provide a blueprint for living with love, integrity, and purpose. This book presents five foundational lessons:

Radical Love That Breaks Barriers

Jesus called us to love not only our neighbors but even our enemies. This bold compassion demonstrates an extension of His grace when least expected—and most needed.

Forgiveness That Sets You Free

Forgiving others is not only a gift to them—it is a path to personal healing and peace. Jesus taught that forgiveness gives freedom from bitterness and pain.

True Greatness Through Humble Service

In word and deed, Jesus revealed that real greatness comes from serving others. His life was a masterclass in humility, posing a challenge to believers to lead with love, not ego.

Faith That Shows Up in Action

Jesus clearly said that faith is not only what we say but also how we live. Through kindness, generosity, and justice, we reflect the heart of God in everyday moments.

A Kingdom Worth Seeking

Jesus spoke of a spiritual kingdom founded on love, mercy, and righteousness—a realm not of earthly power, but of eternal purpose. He called us to seek lasting values over temporary gain, inviting hearts to pursue what truly endures.

Unconditional Love

Unconditional love is the foundation of living a life with Jesus. We are called to strive to walk as He did. Jesus helped everyone without distinction,and held the same view of all people.

Unconditional love isn't merely a virtue—it's the very heartbeat of Jesus' ministry. It's the foundation for a life shaped by His character, guided by His compassion, and aligned with His calling. To walk with Jesus is to live in the light of that love, striving each day to reflect the grace He freely gives to all.

Jesus' love was not selective. He never judged anyone based on status, appearance, ability, or past mistakes. He saw each person as precious and worthy of healing, hope, and restoration. Regardless of circumstance or background, His response remained the same unwavering love, compassion, and grace.

Walking like Jesus is loving like Jesus—not only when it is easy, not only when someone agrees with us. We love like Jesus especially when it is hard—when the world deems someone unworthy, when instincts lean toward judgment, and when hearts are weary. In these moments, unconditional love becomes a radical act of faith.

The Scripture clearly states, "For God does not show favoritism." (Romans 2:11). In other words, God does not play favorites—He treats everyone with equal love and fairness. Jesus lived this truth by never judging people based on wealth, status, appearance, or past mistakes. He did not elevate one group above another; instead, He looked beyond the surface and into the heart of each person. Jesus never showed unfair bias or preference toward anyone. His love was steady, compassionate, and extended to all.

In a world obsessed with comparison, Jesus invites us to view it through a different lens—love—and to recognize that every person, regardless of ability, background, or circumstance, was made in the image of God.

God is Light

The word "light" was mentioned in the Bible approximately 260 times, depending on the translation. It remains one of the most powerful and recurring symbols used to describe:

God's Presence and Glory: (1 John 1:5)

"This is the message we have heard from him and declare to you: God is light; in him there is no darkness at all."

Truth and Revelation: (John 8:12)

When Jesus spoke again to the people, he said, "I am the light of the world. Whoever follows me will never walk in darkness, but will have the light of life."

Wisdom and Guidance: (Psalm 119:105)

"Your word is a lamp for my feet, a light on my path."

Salvation and Hope: (Isaiah 9:2).

"The people walking in darkness have seen a great light; on those living in the land of deep darkness a light has dawned."

Christian Witness: (Matthew 5:14–16)

"You are the light of the world. A town built on a hill cannot be hidden. Neither do people light a lamp and put it under a bowl. Instead they put it on its stand, and it gives light to everyone in the house. In the same way, let your light shine before others, that they may see your good deeds and glorify your Father in heaven."

The Bible says, "God is light, and in Him is no darkness at all." This statement is not only a theological truth—it is a spiritual lens for how we live, think, and become. Light reveals, heals, and guides, whereas darkness distorts, hides, and misleads. When we walk in the light of God, we align with truth, clarity, and purpose.

Walking in the Light

From the beginning, my work—serving people by providing computer products and services—has been rooted in a simple, powerful truth found in (1 John 1:5–7). This is the foundation I live by:

(1 John 1:5–7) "This is the message we have heard from him and declare to you: God is light; in him there is no darkness at all. If we claim to have fellowship with him and yet walk in the darkness, we lie and do not live out the truth. But if we walk in the light, as he is in the light, we have fellowship with one another, and the blood of Jesus, his son, purifies us from all sin."

This verse means no hate, no prejudice, no negative feelings toward anyone. Every person is created equally with a heart, a soul, and a purpose. Their appearance, their abilities or the lack thereof—they are all irrelevant. What matters is that every person deserves love.

People are shaped by their thoughts. In turn, our thoughts are shaped by what we see, hear, and read. Our minds are not isolated—they are influenced by every input we allow in. Exposure becomes experience, experience becomes belief, and belief ultimately becomes behavior.

(Garbage In, Garbage Out) is a term in software programming that means that flawed input leads to flawed output. The same principle applies to our minds and hearts. If we feed our brains with negativity, confusion, or deception, then our thoughts and actions will reflect them. But, if we feed our minds with truth, love, and light, then we become vessels of clarity and compassion.

Your brain is the hardware, while your mind is the software. And the spirit—it is the power source. When God's light is your input, then grace, wisdom, and peace becomes your output.

You Are the System—Guard Your Inputs

Similar to a computer, your body has hardware (the brain) and software (the mind). In contrast to machines, however, the soul is eternal—and the spirit is inclined toward the light. The inputs you allow—what you see, hear, read, and dwell on—influence your thoughts, emotions, and, ultimately, actions.

The Bible says, "God is light, and in Him is no darkness at all." To walk in this light, we must guard our gates—the sensory portals that feed our inner world. GIGO is not only a programming principle but also a spiritual truth.

Controlling Your Inputs

Here are practical, faith-aligned ways to filter what input enters your mind and heart:

*Opt for uplifting media: Watch films, shows, and videos that reflect hope, truth, and compassion.

*Avoid toxic imagery: Avoid content that glorifies violence, lust, or despair.

*Surround yourself with beauty: Art, nature, and Scripture-based visuals can renew the spirit.

Auditory Input (Hearing)

*Fill your ears with faith: Listen to Christian artists and stations that share uplifting, hope-filled music grounded in Biblical truth.

*Turn down the noise: Steer clear of gossip, profanity, and fear-based chatter that clouds the spirit.

* Speak life daily: Your words shape your mindset—choose affirmations rooted in the Scripture to renew the heart and mind.

Cognitive Input (Reading and Learning)

*Pick up the Bible and read the Word daily: The Scripture is the ultimate antivirus—it renews the mind and protects the heart.

*Choose edifying books and articles: Seek wisdom, testimonies, and teachings that align with God's truth.

*Be mindful of social media: Curate your feed to reflect light instead of chaos.

Emotional Input (Environment and Relationships)

*Surround yourself with light-bearers: Fellowship with believers who respect you as a person and uplift and challenge you in love.

*Practice mindfulness and prayer: These practices help you recognize intrusive thoughts and replace them with the truth.

*Create a sanctuary: Your home, workspace, and digital spaces should reflect peace and purpose.

Guard Your Input

Carry yourself with confidence—not with arrogance, but with the quiet strength that comes from knowing your identity in Jesus Christ. Stay strong in spirit and alert in mind, constantly aware of what enters your heart and thoughts. Every moment brings new input—what you see, hear, feel, and experience—and each one holds the power to shape your mindset, choices, and character.

To live in the light, you must protect the gateways to your soul. Be deliberate, stay mindful, and anchor yourself in truth. When you find yourself surrounded by negativity or darkness, pause, take a breath, and ask yourself: "What would Jesus do?" He embodied love—unwavering, patient, and inclusive. Let this be your guide.

Final Thought: What You Take in, You Give Out

You are not only a receiver—you are also a transmitter. What you allow into your heart and mind will eventually shape your words, actions, and outlooks. When your spirit is tuned to faith, your life begins to echo grace, wisdom, and love. Walking in the light is not only possible—it becomes natural.

Prayer is our way of speaking to God.

The Scripture is God's way of speaking to us.

Therefore, guard your input, feed your soul with truth, and let your life reflect the light of Jesus!

Hand-in-Hand with Jesus

Being saved is not the end—it is the beginning of a journey. We grow in faith, serve others, and reflect Christ's love. Although we stumble, we are never alone, because God's grace carries us.

This book is a guide for walking through life hand-in-hand with Jesus Christ, learning to view the world through His eyes, and embracing the blessings we have been called to share with others. It is not only about receiving grace but also about becoming a vessel of grace. When we help others with their needs, we discover that God has already prepared what we need in return. His provision is perfect, timely, and tailored to our hearts.

The Blessing of Giving

Jesus taught that the greatest among us is the servant of all. When we lift others up, we are lifted. When we open our hands to give, we also open our hearts to receive.

(Luke 6:38) reminds us of the following: "Give, and it will be given to you. A good measure, pressed down, shaken together and running over, will be poured into your lap. For with the measure you use, it will be measured to you."

Life Is a Choice

Every day presents a crossroad. We can choose to open doors for others—doors of opportunity, encouragement, and healing—or we can walk past them—too busy or too burdened to notice. We can choose gratitude by saying "thank you" when someone shows us kindness, or we can let the moment pass in silence. These choices shape our character and reflect the heart of Jesus Christ within us.

The Call to Love Equally

Jesus' love was not selective. He embraced the outcast, healed the broken, and welcomed the forgotten. His command is clear:

(John 13:34) "A new command I give you: Love one another. As I have loved you, so you must love one another."

In this verse, Jesus talks about loving without condition, bias, and hesitation. It means helping those in need—not only when it is convenient, but whenever we can. Whether through a word of encouragement, a helping hand, or a quiet prayer, we are called to be present, compassionate, and generous.

Life with Jesus is active, intentional, and deeply relational. It is about choosing love and service and trusting that God will meet every need as we walk in obedience and grace.

Life is Full of Choices

You can open a door for someone, or walk past without a thought. You can say "thank you" when kindness is shown, or stay silent. Every moment offers a decision.

Jesus teaches us to love all people equally and to serve those in need whenever we are able. His example reminds us that compassion is not only a feeling—it is an action. Importantly, every small choice can be a reflection of His love.

The command to love your neighbor is found in several places in the Bible, but it was first mentioned in the Old Testament: (Leviticus 19:18): "Do not seek revenge or bear a grudge against anyone among your people, but love your neighbor as yourself. I am the Lord."

Jesus later elevates it as one of the greatest commandments: (Mark 12:31): The second is this: 'Love your neighbor as yourself.' There is no commandment greater than these."

These passages demonstrate that love is not merely a moral suggestion—it is a divine command.

Jesus made it clear that loving God and loving others are inseparable. It is not optional or secondary; it is the core of faith. Truly loving God denotes reflecting His love in how we treat people—especially when it is inconvenient, uncomfortable, or undeserved. It is a call to live with compassion, humility, and grace, because that is how He loves us.

The Romans Road to Salvation

The Romans Road is a powerful, straightforward means of sharing the message of salvation using key verses from the Book of Romans. It is not a physical road, but a spiritual journey—a step-by-step guide through the Scripture that reveals how one can be saved and born again through faith in   Jesus Christ.

Path to Salvation

1. We are all sinners (Romans 3:23) "For all have sinned and fall short of the glory of God."
None of us are perfect, and we have all missed the mark of God's holiness.

2. The consequence of sin is death (Romans 6:23) "For the wages of sin is death, but the gift of God is eternal life in Christ Jesus our Lord."
Sin separates us from God—but He offers eternal life as a free gift.

3. God showed His love through Jesus (Romans 5:8) "But God demonstrates His own love for us in this: While we were still sinners, Christ died for us." Jesus did not wait for us to clean up our lives—He gave His life for us at our worst.

4. Salvation comes through faith (Romans 10:9) "If you declare with your mouth, "Jesus is Lord," and believe in your heart that God raised him from the dead, you will be saved." This passage speaks about relationship, instead of religion. Faith in Jesus brings salvation.

5. Call on Him and be saved (Romans 10:13) "Everyone who calls on the name of the Lord will be saved. This promise is for everyone regardless of your past, pain, or position.

Final Thoughts: Prayer with Purpose

As you continue navigating life with Jesus, let prayer be your compass—daily, intentional, and aligned with your purpose. Prayer is not just a ritual; it's a relationship. It's where your heart meets His will, where your goals are refined by grace, and where your steps are strengthened by faith. When you begin each day in prayer, you're not just asking—you're aligning. You're inviting God to walk with you, guide you, and empower you to pursue what He's placed in your heart.

Let your prayers reflect your goals. Speak to God about your dreams, your challenges, your calling. Ask boldly, listen humbly, and move forward with confidence. When your prayers and your plans walk hand in hand, you'll find clarity, courage, and divine momentum. You'll begin to see not just progress, but purpose in every step.

In my own work helping people, I begin each visit with prayer. Before I step out of my car, I ask God for wisdom—to truly listen to my customers, understand their needs, and serve them with excellence. And when the visit is done, I return to my car and pray again—this time for their success, that the technology I've provided will empower them, uplift them, and help them live with greater independence and joy. These prayers are not just habits; they are my way of staying connected to the mission and the people I serve.

And always remember the promise of Jesus in (Mark 11:24):

"Therefore I tell you, whatever you ask for in prayer, believe that you have received it, and it will be yours."

Believe it. Receive it. Live it. Jesus is with you—every step, every breath, every battle.

A Prayer for the Reader of this Book

Lord Jesus, thank you for walking with me through every chapter of life—through valleys of doubt and peaks of joy, through seasons of waiting and moments of revelation. You have been my compass when I was lost, my strength when I was weary, and my peace when the world felt loud. I praise You for Your mercy that never runs dry and Your grace that meets me right where I am.

Help us, Lord, to navigate life with You—not only in major decisions, but in quiet, daily choices that shape who we become. Teach us to forgive quickly, to love deeply, and to serve humbly. Let our homes be places of healing and hope, our work rooted in purpose, and our faith more than words—let it be a living testimony. When storms come, anchor us. When blessings overflow, keep us grateful. When we forget, gently remind us that You are always near.

Amen.

The Legacy of a Full Boat

And when the journey nears its end,

may your boat be full—not of possessions, but of moments.

Moments of laughter shared, burdens lifted, hands held, and hearts opened.

May your wake leave ripples of kindness,

and your sails bear marks of resilience and grace.

You may not have chosen every storm,

but you chose to keep sailing.

You may not have had every answer,

but you offered love—even when the map was vague.

And this love—quiet, steady, enduring—

is the legacy that will outlast the voyage.

So let the final stretch be one of peace.

Let forgiveness be your anchor.

Let gratitude be your compass.

Let your story remind others

that even an empty boat can carry light.

Because the greatest journeys are not measured by distance,

but by the lives we touch along the way.